Life wasn't meant to be easy.
But take courage, child – for it can be delightful.

George Bernard Shaw (1856 – 1950)

Noble deeds and hot baths are the best cures for depression.

Dodie Smith (1896 – 1990)

Lucky Duck is more than a publishing house and training agency. George Robinson and Barbara Maines founded the company in the 1980s when they worked together as a head and as a psychologist, developing innovative strategies to support challenging students.

They have an international reputation for their work on bullying, self-esteem, emotional literacy and many other subjects of interest to the world of education. George and Barbara have set up a regular news-spot on the website at:
 http://www.luckyduck.co.uk/newsAndEvents/viewNewsItems
and information about their training programmes can be found at:
www.insetdays.com

More details about Lucky Duck can be found at:
http://www.luckyduck.co.uk

Visit the website for all our latest publications in our specialist topics

- Emotional Literacy
- Bullying
- Circle Time
- Asperger's Syndrome
- Self-esteem
- Positive Behaviour Management
- Anger Management
- Eating Disorders

How to use the CD-ROM

The CD-ROM contains a PDF file labelled 'Worksheets.pdf' which contains worksheets for each session in this resource. You will need Acrobat Reader version 3 or higher to view and print these pages.

The document is set up to print to A4 but you can enlarge the pages to A3 by increasing the output percentage at the point of printing using the page set-up settings for your printer.

To photocopy the worksheets directly from this book, set your photocopier to enlarge by 125% and align the edge of the page to be copied against the leading edge of the copier glass (usually indicated by an arrow).

Foreword

This book was originally published in Australia and was intended for young people to work through alone.

I liked its humorous, punchy style and with the authors' permission have amended it to suit delivery in schools, youth groups, social service provision – in fact anywhere that adults and young people interact in formal or informal situations.

I have tried to ensure its flexible approach has not been lost. It will provide resources that engage young people and generate healthy and sometimes heated debate.

George Robinson

Contents

How to Use the Material

The format has been kept very open-ended to allow ease of use across both formal and informal environments. The chapters can be developed and the time spent on each chapter's theme can be varied to suit the group.

Within the structure of the programme there are five habits that are continually practised:

1) Being calm.
2) Having energy.
3) Having courage.
4) Giving care.
5) Making plans.

The programme starts with an exploration of these areas and each theme incorporates the five habits.

All of the habits are linked to each other. Each small change you make to one habit will cause changes to other habits. Improving one habit will make the others stronger.

This programme tells you how to master these habits. Then it tells you how to use them to master three of the most common emotions: anger, worry and helplessness. These are the emotions that are most likely to cause difficulty for people who allow them to get out of control.

Rather than provide a prescriptive format the programme offers:

▸ Facilitator's guidelines regarding what might be said to introduce the various activities.

▸ Worksheets to photocopy (or print) for the young people to complete.

▸ Discussion and feedback regarding activities and points raised. These sections are highlighted by the lips icon:

Recording the young people's work

The most important element is the process of thinking, reflecting and discussion. You may think that it is important for the young people to keep a record of their work.

We suggest the participants are provided with a ring file or similar to be able to keep their work in a way that reflects the importance of this programme and their contribution. In the appendix we have provided examples of front covers for their folders that could be provided for young people to complete, but this age group might prefer to design their own front cover.

You might be faced with groans of disappointment with the mention of worksheets. The worksheets are of a magazine approach of circling the appropriate answers and the group should find them engaging.

Finally, don't feel you must follow our suggested format, use the materials to suit your group.

Important: The tests used throughout the book are not clinically diagnostic tests. They are designed to help young people understand the meaning of the emotion in question. They may also indicate to young people whether their thinking style is optimistic or pessimistic. If any person has concerns about her answers, she should seek assistance from a trained professional.

Evaluation of Sessions

To involve young people in the process of reflection you might think it important to provide some vehicle for evaluation. This could be done in a variety of ways. As we have kept the format open-ended, when you evaluate will depend on how much of each of them you have covered.

Discussion at the end of the session

Questions posed could include:

▸ What was the best part of the session?
▸ What was the worst part of the session?
▸ What have I learned?
▸ What am I going to think about?
▸ What might I change about me?

This could either be done as a group or pair/small group work with some feedback at the end.

Evaluation

Providing an evaluation form that allows the young people to respond individually is more appropriate for some groups. The evaluation sheets can be a personal record of how the programme has affected the individual. In the appendix there is an open-ended evaluation form that can be used at any stage of the programme.

There should be an opportunity for some group feedback. This format allows individuals to make a personal comment without having to disclose their feelings to either another individual or the group.

Taking negative feedback

One of the five habits focused on is having courage. If this is an essential element of the programme then you must allow the young people to have the courage to provide negative feedback and you must have the courage to accept it.

In Search of Inner Peace: Being Calm

Calm brings peace to the heart and clarity to the mind. When calm, a person is free from agitation and disturbance.

Calm people have self-awareness. They become more aware of themselves and their emotions.

Introduce the idea of emotions and feelings. Different situations have different effects on us but people also respond to situations in different ways.

Rate Your Emotional Profile

Tick the box that shows how often you feel these emotions.

Emotion	Never	Sometimes	Often
happy			
angry			
lonely			
loving			
helpless			
hateful			
excited			
calm			
bored			
worried			
energetic			
joyous			
belonging			
satisfied			
powerful			
confident			

What are your favourite emotions?

_____

_____

_____

_____

What are your least favourite emotions?

_____

_____

_____

_____

Only when you begin to understand yourself will you begin to understand other people. Once you begin to understand others, life will become easier. What did you notice from your answers?

Calm People Accept Who They Are

Calm people learn to accept who they are. They acknowledge and then they try to understand and control their feelings. They attempt to use their feelings as their ally, rather than despise them as their enemy.

Acceptance does not mean you have to limit yourself. After all, remember that Beethoven was deaf! Acceptance requires you to be aware of those things you can change and those things that you cannot change.

Tick the relevant column, yes, no or sometimes in answer to the statement, 'Things you can change'.

Things you can change	Yes	No	Sometimes	Things you can change	Yes	No	Sometimes
body shape				sexual preference			
moods				grief			
worry				talent			
performance				feeling helpless			
energy				fear			
migraine				asthma			
happiness				death			
behaviour				wealth			
parents				anger			
friends				drug use			
marks at school				feelings			
attitudes				religion			
tastes in music				war			
injustice				appetite			
flatulence				hobbies			

Calm people learn to accept those things they cannot change. Those people who fail to accept what they cannot change are forever frustrated. What did you notice from your answers?

Impulse control

Calm people develop the skill of impulse control. Impulse control is the ability to control your urges, usually because if you don't, something bad might happen.

Somebody stands on your toe when you are climbing Mount Everest. Your impulse is to pull your foot away. If you do you might fall off the ledge to your death. You control your impulse and save yourself. This is impulse control in the extreme.

A police officer stops you when you are walking along the street. He is suspicious. He asks questions hinting you have done something wrong. Your impulse is to tell him your feelings, perhaps coloured with a few expletives. But you realise the police officer has more power than you. The short-term satisfaction of telling the police officer your thoughts may cause more serious consequences. So you keep your thoughts to yourself. This is impulse control.

How to practise being calm

Unless you become a monk or a hermit you are unlikely to always be calm. Life is too difficult. But then again, because life can be difficult, you need to be as calm as possible. By taking time each day to feel calm, you will find the rest of your day becomes calmer.

The following simple activities are ways of practising how to calm yourself. You might like to take some time each day to practise them.

Two common ways people learn to be calm is through practising relaxation and meditation. If you feel confident with the group get them to do the next three activities.

How to really relax

You lie on the floor with your eyes closed. You begin with your toes. Tense them as tight as possible and then loosen them completely. Keep them loose. Then tense your feet as tight as possible and then loosen them. Keep them loose. Tense your calf muscles as tight as possible, and then loosen them. Keep them loose.

Work up through your whole body, until you feel relaxed, like jelly.

How to meditate

Find a comfortable position, either cross-legged or lying down. You might need some help with meditation. The aim is to clear your mind of thought. Without thought, you will be calm. Clearing your mind of thought is very difficult. Thoughts keep creeping back into it. Some people have a mantra they repeat to themselves. The mantra helps to block out other thoughts. Aim to meditate for twenty minutes.

So Hum

So Hum is a yoga method for focusing the mind, and is useful when feeling stress. Sit in a chair with your backside back in the chair so that you are sitting fairly upright. Place your hands in your lap. Either close your eyes or focus them on one of your hands. Breathe easily in and out through your nose. As you breathe in say silently to yourself, "So," and as you breathe out, say slowly to yourself, "Hum."

Being calm

Discuss with the students ways they use to feel calm.

Remember that sometimes you might get responses that are intended to be challenging and provocative. Part of this programme is about being courageous.

Responses might include:

- sex
- smoking (legal and illegal substances)
- drugs
- alcohol.

Consider your responses but in discussion see whether the group has worries about these in terms of good and bad choices of relaxing. It's probably best as the facilitator to avoid judgements but giving factual information is okay.

Habit builders

- Listening to peaceful music with your eyes closed.
- Doing Tai Chi.
- Jogging.
- Shopping without any money.
- Fiddling with your bike.

- Having a massage.
- Daydreaming.
- Writing poetry to your crush.
- Walking the dog.
- Reading quietly and alone.
- Floating in water.
- Singing, humming and whistling.
- Having a bath with lavender oil.
- Patting your pet snake.
- Taking a nap.
- Going to church.
- Looking at your baby pictures in a photo album.
- Drinking water.
- Thinking pleasant thoughts.
- Giving a compliment.
- Helping someone.
- Knitting or sewing.
- Drawing cartoons of your teachers.
- Going for a long distance jog or swim.

The Elixir of Life: Having Energy

People fall into two categories, those who are passive and those who are proactive.

Passive people

Passive people tend to respond to things as they happen. They live from day to day and are more prone to follow the crowd. People who are completely passive have little control over their lives. Opportunities and circumstances control them. They wander through life gradually being sapped of energy.

Proactive people

Proactive people are positive. They tend to be initiators, working to make things happen. They plan ahead and are more prone to making independent decisions, often becoming leaders. People who are proactive have control over their lives. They work to shape their opportunities and circumstances. They set their own course in life and gain energy and momentum as they advance.

Imagine being madly in love with a crush who never notices you. The passive person is resigned to their fate. They live in hope that their crush will one day notice them. They daydream about how things might be. The proactive person makes sure they are noticed. They say hello to their crush and smile, they send gifts and give compliments and they sing love songs and do handstands at school assemblies. Well, perhaps the love songs and handstands are going too far. Proactive people do not have to be exhibitionists, but wherever possible, they do need to try to take control of their destiny.

Imagine you are angry. A friend is calling you by a name you do not like. The passive person will keep quiet and hope they stop. The proactive person will tell them they do not like it, think up smart responses, come up with equally 'complimentary' names or whatever else might get the message across. What might happen if the passive person did nothing? Could the proactive person make the situation worse?

Most people are somewhere between being passive and proactive. They tend to be proactive about things that are important to them and perhaps more passive when things are of lesser importance.

Which things are you proactive about?

- Schoolwork
- Crushes
- Designer labels
- Hairstyles
- Family issues
- Sport
- Health and fitness
- Beliefs
- Solving problems
- Social life

Can you be specific? Clarify what you do in these situations that makes you proactive.

Being positive

Being positive gives people energy. When your friend gets rejected on a date, a positive person might give encouragement by saying something like, 'They don't realise what they just missed out on.'

Saying something reassuring and trying to look on the positive side will build a person up and give them energy. If you are in the habit of saying positive things to other people, you are more likely to say positive things to yourself. You will be a bright spark!

Being negative

On the other hand, saying negative things robs people of energy. A negative comment to a rejected friend might be, 'Let's face it, you were playing way out of your league.'

Being negative is a miserable way to live. If you say negative things to other people, you are more likely to say them to yourself.

Eventually, people avoid negative types. They know negative people are like prowling sharks waiting to drag people down. Energy sappers!

Of course, some days it is easier to be positive than on other days. Being positive requires effort, especially in some situations, like when you accidentally overdose on the hair colouring or you wake up to a large boil on your nose.

So how can you be a bright spark?

Being positive does not come naturally. You have to practise. And you need encouragement. That is why you should encourage your friends to be positive. Challenge them if they are being negative about everything. Stop yourself from being too critical.

At first it takes a lot of effort, but as time goes by, you will find that being positive comes more easily. Try it. You will feel better about life.

And amazingly, often life actually does get better.

Positive Thinking

List three positive things about yourself.

1) _____
2) _____
3) _____

List three positive things about your friend.

1) _____
2) _____
3) _____

Now for the big test. List three positive things about your teacher or an adult you are working with.

1) _____
2) _____
3) _____

Remember it's often easier to be negative than positive.

Is your glass half full or half empty?

Decisions and Dilemmas – Facing the Avalanche!

Each day we make small decisions to resolve the hundreds of dilemmas we face. Many of these decisions we barely notice. Here are examples of some of these dilemmas. What could the decisions be? Fill in the boxes.

Common Dilemmas	Common Decisions
When will I get up?	
When will I go to school?	
What do I want for lunch?	
What will I have for lunch?	
What is my plan after school?	
What do I decide to do after school?	
Should I do the dishes after the meal?	
What time will I go to bed?	
What will I watch on TV?	

Avalanche!

Sometimes you have too many dilemmas, and too many decisions to make. You might feel like you are being overwhelmed by an avalanche. This might cause feelings you could do without, like worry and helplessness. If you do not try and take control, you find yourself stressed and unable to act.

In times like these you need to:

▸ Calm yourself.
▸ Write down all of your dilemmas.
▸ Rate them from 'highest priority' to 'lowest priority'.
▸ Make one decision at a time.

When decisions are too difficult:

Find out more information

If you do not feel ready to make a decision, put it in the 'too hard basket' and come back to it later. If it will help, try and get some more information to make the decision easier. For instance, when deciding whether you want a job serving hamburgers, you might not be able to decide until you know the pay rates and the hours of work. When deciding whether you will do your homework, you might need to check the television guide.

Discuss with someone

Some decisions are difficult to make alone. You need another person's opinion. They might help you to sort through your ideas. They might have information that will help. They might give an opinion. They might come up with alternatives you have not considered. Or they might just give you confidence.

Review

Your first decision is not always the best decision. You are allowed to make mistakes. Be prepared to revisit your decisions and change them if necessary.

Consciously making decisions will help to give you control over your life. Your stress will fall. Your energy will increase.

Energy Booster Quiz

Allow the young people to complete the quiz: the answers might provide a basis for interesting discussion.

Answers

A predominance of (a) and/or (c) answers indicate that you are doing a lot of energy sapping. It may eventually catch up with you. Try changing some of those energy-sapping habits towards energy boosting. You will notice the difference.

A predominance of (b) and/or (d) answers indicate that you are doing your best to keep your energy levels boosted. Having energy helps you to achieve your goals, cope with stress and generally enjoy life.

Sorting Out the Chaos

Rate these dilemmas in order of priority.
(1 being the most important and 15 the least important).

	Should I have a glass of water?
	Will I go for a walk?
	Will I do my homework?
	Where will I live when I leave home?
	How should I ask my parents about going to the party on Saturday?
	What sort of car will I buy when I turn 18?
	Do I want to keep spending money on magazines?
	What sort of job do I want when I leave school?
	Which homework should I do first?
	When should I begin doing my homework?
	Will I ask my crush to the party on Saturday?
	Do I want learn the drums or electric guitar?
	What should I throw at my boss when I quit my job?
	Who will I vote for when I am old enough?
	Do I need to buy some more undies before the party on Saturday?

My Dilemmas

Try listing all of your current dilemmas both large and small.

Can you think of ten? If not, list as many as you can.

1 _____
2 _____
3 _____
4 _____
5 _____
6 _____
7 _____
8 _____
9 _____
10 _____

Now prioritise them from the most important to the least important.

Most important   1 _____
                 2 _____
                 3 _____
                 4 _____
                 5 _____
                 6 _____
                 7 _____
                 8 _____
                 9 _____
Least important 10 _____

Energy Booster Quiz

1. How is your bedroom different from your friends' bedrooms?
    - a) Yours is the room you only ever see in the dark.
    - b) Yours is the one that has everything neatly in its place.
    - c) Yours is the one with a week's laundry mixed with magazines strewn all over the floor.
    - d) Yours is the one with the cool posters and the incense burning.

2. How would you describe your eating habits?
    - a) You snack on junk food while hanging out with friends, or, you don't eat because it interferes with your social life.
    - b) You eat three healthy meals a day.
    - c) You like anything you can heat quickly in the microwave.
    - d) You eat lots of fruit and vegetables.

3. Why do you mostly consume liquids?
    - a) To quench your thirst.
    - b) You like the taste.
    - c) To get drunk.
    - d) To be healthy.

4. Why do you smoke, drink alcohol or use other recreational drugs?
    - a) You're addicted.
    - b) You don't.
    - c) To annoy your parents/carers.
    - d) To be sociable.

5. Why do you have a job?
    - a) To pay for your cigarettes.
    - b) You don't.
    - c) To impress your friends with all of your money.
    - d) To fill your time and to make new acquaintances.

6. Why do you listen to music?
    - a) It's more fun than studying.
    - b) To feel good.
    - c) It's better than sleeping.
    - d) To add to my cool image.

Energy Booster Quiz – continued

7. What television shows do you like?
    - a) Anything and everything.
    - b) None.
    - c) All of the latest soaps.
    - d) Sports, movies and/or music clips.

8. How do you tend to sleep?
    - a) Staring at the ceiling.
    - b) Well enough to keep my good looks.
    - c) Like a boat in a rough sea.
    - d) Like a baby.

9. What do you like talking to your friends about?
    - a) I don't have any friends.
    - b) Sports and/or shopping.
    - c) Things that nobody else wants to talk about like, 'How exciting the last science class was!'
    - d) Relationships and feelings.

10. How do you relax?
    - a) By sitting down in front of the television.
    - b) By doing Tai Chi.
    - c) By having a smoke.
    - d) By listening to music and flipping through magazines.

Count your responses

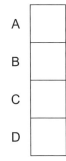

A	
B	
C	
D	

Energy Boosters and sappers – habit builders

You sometimes have days when you feel flat and low on energy for no reason. Everything else seems fine, but you just can't get into things. Being human means that you sometimes think of your brain and body as separate things – but they are not. If you haven't eaten or slept properly, done any exercise or had a laugh, your brain will be just as out of shape as your body.

Energy comes in many disguises and, like magic, can just as easily vanish. To protect your energy levels, have a think about the following energy boosters and sappers.

Food and water

Food and water gives energy. To have peak energy, you must feed yourself well. So what is good food? A healthy diet varies from one person to another. You need to experiment and discover what most suits your needs. Here are some facts to think about when planning your diet.

▶ Eat loads of fruit and vegetables, both with meals and in between meals.

▶ Protein is an essential part of your diet. Meat, fish, nuts, milk, yoghurt and cheese are all high in protein.

▶ How much of your body is water? 10%, 50% or over 70%? We will give you a hint. Most of your brain and body is water. The answer is 72%. You need to avoid running yourself dry. Sip plenty of water throughout the day. Lots of people carry a bottle. Some even give their bottle a name!

▶ Avoid too many cups of tea and coffee.

▶ Fad diets do not work unless you are prepared to stay on them forever.

Recreational drugs

Recreational drugs are those drugs people take for enjoyment. Excessive use of any drug will make you tired and listless. Avoid recreational drugs if you want to perform at your best. If you are not prepared to avoid drugs, decide how you might use them, so they have the least impact on your goals. If you find you cannot make a plan and stick to it when it comes to using drugs, they are beginning to control you, rather than you controlling them.

Recreational drugs have ruined many dreams.

Employment

Too much work and no play will make Jack a dull boy and Jill a dull girl. Having a job while at school is a good source of money and experience. But too much work will sap your energy. Do not overdo it. Make sure you put aside time each day to do something calming that you enjoy.

Television

Try to keep television watching to no more than one or two hours per day. Decide what you want to watch and turn the television on for that show only.

Exercise

Double your normal heart rate through exercising at least four times per week for at least thirty minutes.

People and other animals

You may notice that some people make you feel happy and calm, while other people make you feel tired and stressed. Some people give you energy while others take your energy away from you.

Think of some people you know and ask yourself how you feel after spending time with each of them. Weaker or stronger, better or worse, flat or happy?

Try and spend at least a little time with people who make you feel calm and happy.

Other animals...

'Our perfect companions never have fewer than four feet.'

(Colette, French writer, 1873-1954).

Do you have a pet dog, cat, axolotl or crocodile? Did you know that people who have pets tend to be happier, healthier and more calm than those who don't?

N.B. Crocodile owners may be happier, but they tend to have fewer arms and legs.

Managing the Difficult Emotions

Cont...

If you have a pet (or would like a pet), make a list of what you like about them.

Now make a list of what they like (or would like) about you.

Humour and laughter

'A sense of humour is a sense of proportion.'

(Kahil Gibran, Lebanese poet and mystic)

Humour and laughter prevent us from taking ourselves too seriously. They also produce chemicals in our bodies that both calm us and give us a lift. It is impossible for us to laugh and feel sad at the same time.

Your sense of humour needs practice and exercise. Try spending time with people who laugh and smile. Watch a comedy at least once a week. If you like jokes, try learning a new one each week.

What is funny?

Ask for volunteers to tell a joke.

Humour can be both constructive and destructive. What makes it destructive?

Sleep

Sleeping too much or too little will make you feel tired. Sleeping far too much or far too little can also be a sign that you may be sad or depressed. If this is your sleep pattern over a long time, it may be a good idea to see a doctor.

Talking

Talking makes you feel better. It is as simple as that. When you have bad feelings, talk to someone. When you have good feelings, celebrate with someone.

Enjoyment

Try to build health-promoting activities into your life that you enjoy. Looking forward to something pleasant improves your mental health.

Keep an Energy Booster diary

Keeping an Energy Booster diary for a day will help you to think about your energy levels. You will be able to think about what you are doing well, and what you might want to change.

Energy Booster diary (example)

Time	Energy Booster	Energy Sapper
7.00 am	Woke before the alarm. Fruit, cereal and water for breakfast. Said 'good morning' to mother and smiled.	Yelled at sister. Ignored father.
8.00 am	Packed my bag and checked I had all my books for the day. Left for school in plenty of time. Stopped to admire the weather.	Remembered I had forgotten to do my homework. Thought about how angry the teacher might get. Spent time working out how to dodge class.

Diaries can be a really good way to help individuals reflect on their lives. Though this is the final activity in this section, find some time after students have tried the diary for the day to discuss their records.

You could make mention of some of the well known diarists such as Samuel Pepys, Anne Frank or Alan Clarke and discuss why people spend the time and energy to keep a diary.

Energy Booster Diary

Time	Energy Boosters	Energy Sappers
8.00 – 9.00 am		
9.00 – 10.00 am		
10.00 – 11.00 am		
11.00 – 12.00		
12.00 – 1.00 pm		
1.00 –2.00 pm		
2.00 – 3.00 pm		
3.00 – 4.00 pm		
4.00 – 5.00 pm		
5.00 – 6.00 pm		
6.00 – 7.00 pm		
7.00 – 8.00 pm		
8.00 – 9.00 pm		
9.00 – 10.00 pm		
10.00 – 11.00 pm		
11.00 – 12.00		

Avoiding Decoys: Being Courageous

Having beliefs gives a person something to be courageous about. You have a way of deciding what is right and wrong, just and unjust, fair and unfair. You have a way of deciding what matters and what does not matter.

Beliefs

Having beliefs often leads to making a commitment to what you believe in. This might be about your religion, yourself or the brand of your skateboard.

Imagine you develop a belief in protecting the environment. Your belief is likely to motivate you to behave in an environmentally friendly way. You begin recycling your bottles and papers, you put your rubbish in the bin (even when the teacher asks you to!) and picking up your dog's poo on early evening walks (even when nobody is looking!).

Having beliefs sometimes makes life complicated. Your beliefs may clash with the beliefs of another person. In these circumstances, you need the courage to be understanding and tolerant, while at the same time being careful not to betray yourself.

Risk taking

Risk taking and courage often go hand in hand. Taking risks is an important part of life. Risks help us to discover what we are capable of and to achieve our full potential. Of course risks sometimes turn into disasters. You need to be calculating about them. Learn when the risk is worth taking and when it is not.

Weighing up the risks

Waiting to get on a plane may take a long time and get pretty boring. Jumping from a plane with a parachute might be exhilarating. Jumping from a plane without a parachute is probably suicide. How do we find the balance?

Weighing up the risks is a skill that develops over time. It involves considering:

▸ What is the worst possibility? Am I prepared?

▸ What is the best possibility? Who else could my risk affect?

▸ What is most likely to happen?

Courage and risk taking

Courage can be confusing. Sometimes people think taking risks or being daring is a demonstration of courage, since courage is closely associated with the level of danger attached to whatever the act. Unfortunately, many risks are more stupid than courageous. At best they will achieve nothing of importance, and at worst, someone will get hurt.

Knowing the difference between stupidity and courage is worth learning.

Tolerance

Tolerant people do their best to understand the beliefs of other people. They realise that girls might not always be smarter than boys; that surfing might be cooler than bunji jumping into volcanoes; that the opposition teams might have some talent worth appreciating; and that frozen yoghurt might taste as good as ice cream.

In fact, sometimes, tolerant people discover their own belief was less than one hundred per cent perfect.

Have you ever believed something that you later discovered was wrong?

What's Your Opinion?

Identify whether you think each statement is:

	stupid	courageous	depends
Getting a really bad hairstyle.			
Keeping your crush waiting.			
Arguing with a police officer.			
Starting a petition to change an unfair school rule.			
Driving a stolen car.			
Hitting someone who offended your girl/boyfriend.			
Admitting you are wrong.			
Having unprotected sex.			
Taking a deep breath and walking away when you are angry.			
Keeping quiet rather than hurting someone's feelings.			
Yelling at your parents and storming out.			
Making a plan and sticking to it.			
Trying cannabis.			

Someone you know

Think of someone who has strong beliefs.

Who are they? _____

What do they believe in? _____

How do you know? _____

List some of your beliefs:

_____

_____

_____

Being Courageous – Habit Builders

Rate yourself by circling thte appropriate number.

1 being perfect to 5 being 'I need to do a lot of work'.

	1	2	3	4	5
Making a plan and sticking to it.	1	2	3	4	5
Speaking in public.	1	2	3	4	5
Having an opinion.	1	2	3	4	5
Changing your opinion.	1	2	3	4	5
Having beliefs.	1	2	3	4	5
Being tolerant.	1	2	3	4	5
Forgiving yourself for making a mistake.	1	2	3	4	5
Encouraging yourself after making a mistake.	1	2	3	4	5
Asking a question in class.	1	2	3	4	5
Sticking up for someone.	1	2	3	4	5
Being different from the crowd.	1	2	3	4	5
Learning a new skill.	1	2	3	4	5
Saying 'no'.	1	2	3	4	5
Accepting you're imperfect.	1	2	3	4	5
Controlling your anger.	1	2	3	4	5
Ignoring put downs.	1	2	3	4	5
Being positive.	1	2	3	4	5

What areas are you strong in?

_____

What are you weak at?

_____

What are you going to try and improve?

_____

I plan to:

_____

_____

The Secret of Friendship: Giving Care

Caring people are good friends. They are generous and thoughtful. They practise being calm, they develop habits that protect their energy levels, they have courage and they know the meaning of friendship.

Friendship

Discuss with the group what the qualities are of a good friend and record the answers on a flip-chart or whiteboard.

trustworthy	funny
intelligent	good looking
positive	helpful
kind	trendy
similar interests	good manners
nice parents/ carers	honest
sensitive	cleanliness
easy to talk to	good listener
thoughtful	adventurous
loyal	wealthy
forgiving	friendly to others

Ask individuals to identify the three qualities that are most important to them and to explain why they made their decision.

Being a friend to yourself

To be a good friend to others, you must first be a good friend to yourself. If you are too critical of yourself, or put yourself down, you will be unable to trust your own judgement. If you cannot trust yourself, how could anybody else trust you?

Rather than being negative and sapping yourself of energy, you need to have the courage to learn the lessons that need to be learned, as well as the courage to forgive yourself for errors of judgement. You need to boost yourself up and motivate yourself by saying supportive and encouraging things.

Think about the person who always puts a negative interpretation on things. Nothing is ever right, or good enough, or worth celebrating. They think they are pretty hopeless and everybody else is pretty hopeless as well.

When their friend comes second in a race, they say, 'Don't worry, you'll get over it.'

'What's the problem with that?' you ask.

Perhaps their friend was pleased about coming second. Perhaps they were thinking about what a great race they had run. When their friend says, 'Don't worry, you'll get over it', they begin to have doubts about whether they ran a great race or not. Their great race has been reinterpreted as a failure.

The positive person who knows how to read their friend's feelings senses their satisfaction. They say, 'Great effort. Good on you.'

Alex goes to the movies with a girl he really likes. The girl explains that she is in love with a boy who goes to another school. Alex and the girl talk about what she might do. They enjoy themselves and find it easy to talk to each other.

When Alex tells a friend, his friend says, 'Bad luck. There's plenty more fish in the ocean.'

Alex no longer feels so good about going to the movies with the girl. His friend has just devalued Alex's enjoyment and friendship with the girl.

A friend who shows empathy with Alex and who tries to have positive thoughts might say something like, 'It's a good feeling to be able to talk easily to someone.'

Empathy

When you have empathy with how someone feels, you are more likely to behave in a caring way. Empathy involves trying to put yourself in someone else's shoes and trying to imagine how they might feel. Empathy is an incredibly difficult skill to master because everybody is different. You can never have complete empathy with another person but you can try.

Friends talk

You can guess emotions by watching a person's expressions and reading their body language. But talking is often the best way of knowing how someone is feeling. When someone is telling you about their feelings, they do not necessarily expect you to fix anything. Sometimes they just want to share. So learning to listen intently and ask encouraging questions is a good skill to learn.

Avoid:

- being too quick to give advice
- starting telling your own story
- telling them how they should feel.

Be a calm and intent listener. Wait until the time is right, try to provide encouragement and support and be courageous enough to seek help if needed.

A good way to help other people express themselves is to summarise the feeling they are conveying.

'I had a date with Kate last night and she didn't turn up, didn't phone me... nothing!'

Your answer might be influenced by how this was spoken. 'It sounds like you are upset,' or 'It sounds like you are angry.'

When you ask questions that are open and about feelings you will notice people tend to keep talking. If you practise being an intent listener like this, it will become second nature.

What would you say?

Imagine your friend has missed being included in a school trip to a tropical island where everybody is going scuba diving. All his friends are going, including his girlfriend! You are sitting on a bench together soon after he has been given the bad news.

You say, 'How are you feeling?'

He says, 'What do you think?'

Consider the best response:

a) 'Worried about your girlfriend going off with someone else?'
b) 'Similar thing happened to me once. I got over it.'
c) 'Like hitting someone?'
d) 'I'm not sure how I'd feel.'

Or perhaps you might just sit and wait to see if they wanted to talk.

It is hard to know what you might say, since every situation requires empathy.

What response would be most helpful?

Here is another situation that requires empathy. What would you say in this instance?

Imagine you have just had a drug education class about the dangers of smoking tobacco. Your friend says she is worried about her mother who is a heavy smoker.

You know your friend's father is dead. Her mother has just moved in with another man. Your friend does not like her mother's partner.

You say, 'Why are you worried?'

She says, 'Imagine if mum died.'

Consider the best response:

a) 'She won't die. Only old people die from smoking.'
b) 'If she dies it will be her own stupid fault. Tell her to stop smoking at once.'
c) 'I know exactly how you feel. But don't worry, you will be fine. Trust me.'
d) 'So you are worried about smoking?'

What do you think the friend is really worried about, smoking or the death of her mother? Or perhaps she is worried about what might happen to her. Perhaps she is feeling worried about her mother's new partner.

Open questions

The best way to find out is by asking open questions that keep the conversation going. Having an opinion, whether well intentioned or not, as in (a) and (b), tends to finish the conversation rather than open it up. Telling a person how they feel (c) is another conversation stopper. Whereas (d) is asking your friend to explain more about what they mean and how they feel. It is saying, I am interested and would like to talk about it, but I am not quite sure what you mean.

Ask the students to listen to how people respond. They will hear more of the a/b/c's than the d's.

Seek help

When a problem is too big, a caring person will seek help. Sometimes when a friend tells you about a problem, you won't know what to do. In these instances, it may be worth encouraging them to speak to someone who might be better able to help them. It might take a little time to convince them, but there is plenty of confidential advice available from counsellors, doctors and telephone services that can be found in the telephone directory, or by visiting a local health service.

Who could you talk to when you have problems?

▸ At home.
▸ At school.
▸ About health.
▸ About relationships.
▸ About feeling bad.

Thinking about, 'Why?'

It is difficult to care about other people when they make you angry. Like the person who is always bragging, or the student who always gives stupid answers causing the teacher to explain everything two or three times, or the person who is always late.

In these instances, a caring person will try and think about why the person brags, or gives stupid answers or is always late.

Why do people brag?

a) Because they think they are better than everyone else.
b) Because they want you to like them.
c) Because they care about what you think of them.
d) Because they are lacking in confidence and are trying to build themselves up.

Why do people give stupid answers?

a) Because they want to irritate everybody.
b) Because they are trying to learn.
c) Because they don't know the right answers.
d) Because they don't study hard enough.

Why are some people always late?

a) Because they are inconsiderate.
b) Because they have many responsibilities.
c) Because they are avoiding stress.
d) Because they don't own a watch.

If a person is bragging because they think they are better than everyone else, you might get angrier than if you knew they were bragging because they cared about what you thought of them. Similarly, you might be more patient in class of a person who was trying to learn, than of a person who didn't study hard enough. And finally, it is easier to be angry with a person who is inconsiderate compared to someone with many responsibilities.

By learning to have empathy with others, you learn more about people, their feelings and how to manage them. The irony is that with your new knowledge you will make yourself happy and wiser as well.

'ARKs' – Acts of Random Kindness

If you want to be totally outrageous and unpredictable, make plans to do something kind for a friend, member of your family or even a teacher. Make sure it is totally unexpected, not asked for and totally 'out of the blue'. People will be surprised, shocked, flabbergasted and speechless. And they will also be delighted.

'ARKs' are the way to go!

Think of an 'ARKs' you could do today.

Sending a post card.
Saying 'hello'.
Asking someone about the weekend.
Sharing a smile.
Helping out around the house.
Sharing the last bread roll with your brother.

Think of an ARKs someone could do for you.

The Map of Life: Making Plans

'The difference between a dream and a goal is a plan.' (Anon)

Making a plan is like having a map to guide you. Plans help you to know where you are going in life. They help give the proactive person a sense of direction or purpose. They help you to look at the big picture and to control your emotions.

Delayed gratification

An essential ingredient for achieving a goal is delayed gratification, which is the ability to go without a reward now in order to gain a greater reward later. Delayed gratification is a remarkable skill. It is the ability to shape the future by doing something in the present. It is how we set and achieve goals.

▸ You want to look your best for a date so you go to bed early the night before.

▸ You want a new pair of shoes so you save your money.

▸ You want white teeth so you clean them and avoid smoking.

▸ You want to understand your schoolwork so you pay attention in class and do your homework.

▸ You want to do your best at sport so you exercise and practise.

Impulse control and delaying gratification are difficult skills to develop. But they are necessary to achieving your goals. Achieving goals will help you to have a satisfying and enjoyable life.

What type of goals would you like to achieve?

How would you achieve your goal?

Planning to achieve your goals

A good plan has:

▸ a goal
▸ a time frame
▸ a consideration of the pros and cons

- a plan for overcoming barriers
- a set of strategies to help reach the goal.

General goals are harder to measure than specific goals. Learning to walk on your hands is a specific goal. It can be measured.

'I am going to get more sleep' is a general goal. More sleep than what? How much more sleep? When are you going to get more sleep?

'I am going to go to bed by 10 pm from Sunday to Thursday nights' is a specific goal. It is easy to measure.

Setting goals

Setting goals that can be achieved sounds obvious. But a number of things can interfere with goals. Ask yourself these questions to assess how difficult the goals you have set yourself will be to achieve. The more times you answer 'yes' the more likely your goal is achievable. Pick some goals you would like to achieve.

Can I achieve my goal within a reasonable period of time?

Setting goals too far in the future may sap your energy. Break these goals down into smaller more immediately achievable goals.

'I want to be an actor in the movies' is a goal that may take years.

Breaking it down into a more achievable goal like, 'I am going to join an acting class and attend weekly' is a more immediately achievable goal.

Is my goal realistic?

Deciding whether a goal is realistic requires you to think about:

a) weighing up the pros and the cons
b) the barriers.

The pros of joining an acting class and attending each week might be:

- meeting a new group of friends
- learning new skills
- building confidence
- discovering new talents.

The cons might be:

- the time commitment
- memorising lines
- getting parts you don't like.

You need to decide whether the rewards outweigh the sacrifices.

The barriers might include things like:

- financial cost
- transport to the classes
- waiting lists
- getting permission from your parents/carers.

To make your goal realistic you must plan ways to overcome the barriers. Having plans and back-up plans are useful. For instance, your parents might agree to provide transport. On nights when they are not available, you might ask a friend if you can go with them.

Does my goal rely mainly on myself?

How much you have to rely on other people will limit the control you have over whether your goal is achievable. For instance, the acting school might have screening tests or you might have to rely on your parents to give permission and pay the fees. The more you can rely on yourself, the more control you have over successfully achieving your goal.

So when setting your goals, remember:

- Don't set yourself up for failure.
- Some goals are harder than others and some are impossible.
- Be realistic.

So how will your plan look?

Imagine you have a goal to improve your party tricks. You want to learn to walk on your hands instead of your feet!

How will you learn to do it?

1. You need someone to help. You enlist a friend.
2. You need to build up your upper body strength. You plan an exercise regime.

3. You need to practise your balancing. You need to try walking on your hands with the help of a friend until you can do it without help.
4. You need to refrain from drinking alcohol at parties, since this will muck up your balance.
5. You will need a friend to keep an eye out so you do not walk into anybody. Especially someone who is bigger than you.

Goal: learn to walk on hands.
Time frame: 20 days.

Reality check

In trying to achieve goals it is important to have considered as many elements as possible. Learning to walk on your hands involves many factors. Imagine that is your goal.

What rewards would be received for achieving my goal?

1. Impress friends.
2. Become centre of attention.
3. Unique skill that nobody else can do.
4. Build upper body strength.
5. Become closer friends with Georgie.

What sacrifices must be made?

1. Timetable 30 minutes daily for exercising.
2. Refrain from consuming alcohol at parties.

What might the obstacles and what would the solutions be?

Obstacle	Solution
Convincing Georgie to help	Buy her a present and agree to help her with homework.
Exercising when tired.	Eat plenty of fruit and vegetables, drink water and go to bed by 10pm each night.
Finding weights for bicep curls and bench presses.	Ask the Physical Education teacher for a loan during lunchtimes. Otherwise, join the local gymnasium.

Strategies

What strategies might be needed?

1. Ask Georgie to help.

2. Exercise routine:

> 30 push ups per day.
> 50 leg raises per day.
> Multiple stretching exercises daily.
> 100 bench presses per day.
> 100 bicep curls per day.
> 100 hand squeezes with ball each day.
> Daily gymnastic routine.

3. Hand walking practice with Georgie.
4. Practise going to parties and refraining from alcohol.
5. Check that Georgie likes going to the same parties as me.

Now try and make it specific, set yourself a real goal and try to break it down in the way we have discussed.

Life Map – Habit Builder

Let the young people complete the Life Map.

Life Map: Habit Builder

My name is

_____

My goal is

_____

_____

_____

Commencement date _____

Target date for completion _____

Reality Check

Rewards I will receive for achieving my goal.	Sacrifices I must make to achieve my goal.
1. _____	1. _____
2. _____	2. _____
3. _____	3. _____
4. _____	4. _____

Obstacles/barriers to achieving goal

1. _____

2. _____

3. _____

4. _____

Strategies for achieving goal

1. _____

2. _____

3. _____

4. _____

5. _____

6. _____

The Difficult Emotions

Now that you are aware of 'The Five Habits', you are in good shape to tackle the difficult emotions: worry, anger and helplessness.

Difficult emotions

In the heat of the moment you are taken over by an urge to lash out. Have you ever felt like you are spontaneously erupting? You say something vicious, or hit or push, or stick up your finger, or poke out your tongue. Your actions make the incident worse. Later, you wish you had behaved differently. You regret the trouble and hurt you have caused.

What's the feeling? (Anger.)

Have you ever experienced a time when you were not exercising or taking drugs, that your breath became so hot that you began to sweat and you had a feeling of panic? If it was really serious you might even have become short of breath and felt sick. If you had false teeth, they might have started rattling.

What's the feeling? (Worry.)

Do you ever feel like you are powerless? No matter what you do, nothing works. Everything seems bad. You are completely apathetic. Getting out of bed is an effort!

What's the feeling? (Helplessness.)

Important

You need to remember that the feelings of worry, anger and helplessness are normal. They are felt in varying degrees by every human every day. The reason we are writing this book is to help young people understand their feelings. Especially these three, since they can be more difficult than some of the others. They are the three feelings that cause most emotional ill health. When they are out of control they can cause violence, drug problems, panic attacks and sadness. They can seriously mess up your life.

Spontaneous Eruptions: Anger

What is it?

Anger begins with a thought – 'I am being attacked'.

The body goes into a state of high alert. Alarm bells ring. Mobilisation occurs. War is declared. The body readies itself to defend, attack or retreat, sometimes called 'fight or flight'.

How does it feel?

Muscles tense. Blood pressure and heart rate explode, racing from the head to the arms and legs. You get a surge of heat, your teeth and hands clench, you feel your body get really tight. When you feel this happening, you need to be careful. You might do something you regret.

What happens?

Impulsive people will attack either physically or verbally.

Take time out to regain control.

Anger Quiz Answers

a) answers can get you into trouble.

b) answers make you angrier and more miserable. But don't worry too much, most people behave like this sometimes.

c) answers often turn your anger into sadness. This is the most common way people behave. They get angry, then they get sad. The most important thing is to keep this reaction as short as possible.

d) answers help you to stay calm and solve the cause of the anger. If you can behave like this, you are a very calm person. Also very rare!

Anger Quiz

Circle the answer that best fits your most likely response.

You are at a party and your friend starts teasing you about your secret desires and you:
   a) tell them to shut their mouth
   b) swear under your breath
   c) turn bright red and head for the door
   d) realise they're only trying to be funny.

You jam your finger in a door and you:
   a) yell at the nearest person
   b) yell at the sky
   c) pretend it did not hurt
   d) hold it tight and take deep breaths.

The teacher embarrasses you in front of the class and you:
   a) give a loud commentary to the class about some of the teacher's short-comings
   b) swear under your breath
   c) think nasty thoughts about the teacher
   d) change your behaviour to avoid further criticism.

You are trying to finish an English essay while a student continues to kick the back of your chair and you:
   a) tell them to get lost
   b) give dirty looks
   c) think they are thoughtless
   d) explain to them that they are disturbing you.

Anger Quiz – continued

During breakfast your brother always manages to nick the last piece of toast and you:

      a)   punch him as hard as you can

      b)   complain about unfairness, making yourself more upset as you speak

      c)   storm off to your room

      d)   buy yourself a delicious snack on the way to school.

Total your answers

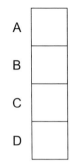

A

B

C

D

Guess what? Do not feel disappointed with your answers. Anger is normal. You cannot stop yourself from feeling anger. But you can learn to control it. Your life will become much easier. You will become angry less often. You will cause fewer problems for yourself!

So how do you control your anger?

The first step is to learn to stop reacting impulsively. Impulsively means doing something without thinking. Practise your impulse control!

Sounds easy? It's very hard. Especially the first few times. But if you can manage to do it, you will feel great.

And don't be miserable if you have a few slip-ups. Keep persevering.

What things work?

Habit builder – four steps to impulse control

1. Take a long and slow breath, then another long and slow breath and another, long and slow. Do not take deep and fast breaths. We do not want you to hyperventilate.

2. Get your muscles to relax and the heat in your face to cool.

3. Block all thoughts. Try counting to ten or doing some other mindless thing in your head (like trying to divide 484 by 26).

4. Encourage and congratulate yourself. It works best if you say it, rather than think it.

When you are calm decide:

What you want to happen.

How to make it happen.

Tooth Rattling: Worry

What is it?

Worry is a warning sign that something is wrong. Worry is the feeling that comes from your search to find all the things that have or might go wrong. You are not always aware of this search. It is going on finding possible problems or dangers. When you identify one, you worry. If worry gets out of control it becomes anxiety, and sometimes depression.

How does it feel?

Worry feels like an empty stomach, shakiness, sleeplessness, feeling distracted, edgy, jumping at shadows and hot breath. If it is really bad it might make you feel sick, give you diarrhoea, headaches, shaky hands and quivering lips. It can stop you from thinking and even speaking. Worry can get right out of control if you do not develop some ways of managing it.

What happens?

When controlled, worry is your friend. It helps protect you from making mistakes, doing bad things and falling into danger.

When out of control, worry is a problem. It makes you sick and unhealthy.

The slippery slope to worry!

You are thinking about asking a girl out on a date. You are considering what might happen. This is the classic path of the tooth-rattling worrier!

You exaggerate how bad or dangerous things might get.

> 'If I ask her out, she will probably laugh at me and tell all her friends I'm a loser!'

You exaggerate how bad or dangerous the consequences could be.

> 'Then as I walk around the school everybody will point at me and chant, 'Loser, Loser, Loser!'

You underestimate your resilience.

> 'I will bow my head and slink off, and eventually be so ashamed I will hide in my bedroom and become a recluse.'

You underestimate those who care about you.

'My friends will forget about me and my parents will despair.'

Worry Quiz Answers

a) answers indicate you probably do not worry enough. If something goes wrong, you won't see it coming.

b) answers indicate that you are controlling your worry, and that it has a positive effect on your life.

c) answers indicate common behaviours that most of us experience from time to time. You will manage to relax and achieve more if you find ways of controlling your worrying. Think about talking to someone you can trust.

d) answers indicate you might become sick if your physical reactions to worry persist. You are advised to speak to someone you trust about your worrying. This might be one of your parents/carers, or a school counsellor or welfare co-ordinator.

Worry Quiz

Circle the answer that best describes you.

How do you tend to sleep?
      a)   staring at the ceiling
      b)   like a boat in a rough sea
      c)   well enough to keep my good looks
      d)   like a baby.

You have been appointed school captain:
      a)   you continue on as normal
      b)   you celebrate
      c)   you become nervous about all that might go wrong
      d)   you are frightened and try to get out of it.

Your best friend gets a new boy/girlfriend:
      a)   you wait and see how long it will last
      b)   you are happy for them
      c)   you know your friendship will never be as good again
      d)   you despair over all the things you won't be able to do together any more.

When you are with other people:
      a)   you behave much the same as when you are alone
      b)   you often enjoy talking and listening
      c)   you change your behaviour so they will like you
      d)   you often feel so self-conscious you can hardly talk.

On Sunday night:
      a)   you rarely think about Monday
      b)   you usually prepare for school
      c)   you often dread Monday morning
      d)   you hyperventilate thinking about what might go wrong in the week ahead.

Count your responses

A ☐   B ☐   C ☐   D ☐

Guess what? Do not feel disappointed with your answers. Worry is normal. You cannot stop yourself from feeling worry. But you can learn to control it. Your life will become much easier. You will have less stress!

So how do you control your worry?

No matter how good or bad things are, most people still worry. So you need to get your worry into perspective. Ask yourself whether it is a big or a little problem. Is it a life changing event, or something that will probably pass unnoticed?

Avoid exaggerating

When you are worried about something, answer the following questions:

What is the worst thing that can happen?

What is the best thing that can happen?

What is the most likely thing that will happen?

Have confidence in yourself

Be positive that things will work out. If they don't, think about ways of coping that are listed in the habit builders in this section.

Have faith in others

Most people are kind and will try to help you out when things go wrong. Most times, all you have to do is ask.

Doing the right thing by Deejay

Without giving it a lot of thought, you plan a party with your friends to celebrate your birthday. That night, another friend (Deejay) rings to wish you all the best. You have been friends since you were young. Your families often go on holidays together. You are still good friends, but you go to different schools. He does not know your other friends and you are unsure what they will think of each other. You fail to give him an invitation.

That night you begin thinking about your party. What if Deejay arrives unexpectedly to give you a present? Or your parents accidentally tell his parents? Deejay will be upset if he finds out, and lying in bed in the middle of the night, it seems highly likely that he will!

That will ruin the end of year holiday. His parents will probably think you are a traitor. They might even decide not to go on holidays any-more. After all those years of being good friends, Deejay might think you are a complete snob and decide to never speak to you again!

So what should you do?

Question: What is the worst thing that could happen?

Answer: Deejay finds out about the party and gets upset. Your friendship is affected.

Question: What is the best thing that could happen?

Answer: The party passes unnoticed.

Question: What is the most likely thing that will happen?

Answer: Whether Deejay finds out or not, your friendship survives. After all, it's hardly a party. It's more like just having a few friends over.

What really happened?

Organising the party was an impulsive decision. Afterwards, you began to realise some of the implications. When you chose not to invite Deejay, you weren't being nasty. You were uncertain about how he would fit in with your other friends. Now that you have had time to think about the possible implications, you are re-considering whether you made the right judgement. Perhaps you could discuss your predicament with your friends, your parents or Deejay. Have faith in others. They might have a helpful idea. If in the worst case scenario, things don't work out, you can always make another plan to show Deejay you are still friends.

Worry – Self Test

Is there something you are worried about at the moment?

Describe what you are worried about

_____
_____
_____

Describe the worst thing that might happen

_____
_____
_____

Describe the best thing that might happen

_____
_____
_____

What do you think will probably happen?

_____
_____
_____

How will you cope with the likely outcome?

_____
_____
_____

Is there someone you trust who you can talk to?

_____
_____
_____

What do you Worry About?

Tick the square that most closely resembles your opinion. Compare your answers with other students.

Worry-wort Richter Scale

	Is absolutely nothing to worry about	There is nothing you can do about it	Is a slight worry	Could cause problems	Indicates a serious personal disaster is looming
Difficulties with teachers					
Conflict with family					
Terrorist attacks					
Failing school					
Smoking cigarettes					
People looking down on you					
Falling out with a friend					
Being overweight					
Getting put down by others					
Being liked					
Getting dumped					

What other things do you worry about?

_____

_____

_____

_____

_____

_____

Problem-solving with Dr W. Wort

Imagine you are Dr W. Wort. You have an advice column in a young people's magazine. What advice would you give?

When you are giving advice to Cindy, Fu, Magda and Dom, ask yourself these questions when deciding what advice you might give:

> What is the problem?
> What is the best outcome?
> How do you achieve the best outcome?
> How do you look after yourself if things don't work out?

Dear Dr W. Wort, My best friend is having a huge sleepover party in a few weeks' time. It is going to be great. Everybody is so excited. But I haven't received an invitation! Here's hoping, Sad Cindy	
Dear Dr W. Wort, I have been playing football since I could walk. I love it. I am 13 years old and have been promoted to the Under 16's team. It is a great opportunity. But I don't want to shower with the older boys after the game. Do you understand what I mean? Very embarrassing, Fu the footballer.	

Problem-solving - continued

Dear Dr W. Wort,

The other day I was borrowing my sister's jacket and I stood on her beloved pet mouse and squashed it. I don't know how to tell her. Especially since I forgot to ask if I could go into her room, or if I could borrow her jacket.

Could it be any worse?
Magda Splat.

_____
_____
_____
_____
_____
_____

Dear Dr W. Wort,

I entered a debating competition with two of my classmates. One thing led to another, and now we are in the regional final. It has become a pretty big deal. Our whole class is coming to watch how we perform. The other day when we were preparing, one of the other team members said I was the weak link. At the time, I thought it was a joke. Now I'm not so sure.

Feeling the pressure,
Doubting Dom.

_____
_____
_____
_____
_____
_____
_____
_____
_____

Give yourself a break

Often, the more you think about a worry, the worse it gets. Sometimes you even start to exaggerate. If you can manage to forget about it for a while, when you think about your worry again, it may not seem as bad.

Clear your mind

Just like when we were discussing anger, being able to clear the thoughts from your mind will help you to relax and stop worrying. Saying or singing reassuring and positive things will also help. It is difficult to have contrary thoughts when you are talking. Reassuring and positive talk will help to block worrying thoughts.

Pleasant worry distracters

What strategies have you found helpful when you are worried?

▸ singing along with your favourite songs
▸ exercising or playing sport
▸ reading
▸ making a healthy meal
▸ watching a movie, especially a funny one
▸ doing homework
▸ cleaning the house
▸ building something
▸ making some clothes
▸ drawing or painting
▸ adventure activities like rock climbing, surfing and canoeing
▸ gardening
▸ playing computer games
▸ helping someone
▸ visiting a friend
▸ visiting an elderly person
▸ going to church
▸ going to an amusement park
▸ bike riding
▸ chopping wood.

Enslavement: Helplessness and Failure

What is it?

Reflecting on the things you do, and the things others do, is how you develop and mature. Sometimes you will feel bad about something you have done, or about something someone else has done. You will think about how you may have acted differently, or perhaps how somebody else should have acted differently. You may even make a judgement about whether an action was fair or unfair, nasty or nice, kind or cruel, a success or a failure. This is all a part of growing and learning. Becoming a fabulously fantastic person.

When reflection becomes too critical and persistent it is dangerous. Thoughts become dishonest and negative. They poison your emotions, causing feelings of failure. The negativity takes away the power to change. One becomes helpless, as if enslaved.

How does it feel?

You think in a negative way, you feel sad and miserable, have difficulty enjoying pleasant activities. In some instances you may behave in a passive and indecisive way, while at other times you might be angry, unco-operative and aggressive. You might even have physical symptoms like pains in the stomach, tiredness, problems with sleeping and headaches.

Helplessness Quiz Answers

a) answers indicate you have a high level of self-confidence. Some might say a little too much, but hey, what the heck. Good on you.

b) answers indicate that you are probably being pretty honest with yourself, but keeping a healthy and positive attitude about who you are and what you might do.

c) answers indicate you are being too hard on yourself. Being negative is a habit that can be broken. When you do, you will enjoy life more than you are at the minute. And remember, the bad times always pass.

d) answers indicate that you are thinking in a way that is unhelpful. Try speaking to someone you trust. If your thoughts persist, seek assistance from a professional. There are many people who are trained to help young people who might be feeling down about themselves or their life.

Helplessness Quiz

Circle the answer that most closely corresponds with your thoughts.

When I think about the future I feel:
- a) happy
- b) optimistic
- c) insecure
- d) miserable

I think other people are better than me:
- a) never
- b) occasionally
- c) often
- d) always

I would prefer to spend the day in bed:
- a) only when I am really sick
- b) after a late night
- c) whenever I have something to do that I would rather avoid
- d) every day of my life.

When I wake up in the morning I look forward to:
- a) everyday things like hanging out with friends, and sometimes, I even look forward to going to school
- b) a special event like the opening of a new movie, a sporting final or a celebration
- c) the end of the week
- d) nothing.

I feel like I always muck things up:
- a) never, or only when something is very difficult
- b) occasionally like when I am in a hurry or when I am tired
- c) whenever I try something new
- d) every day of my life.

Helplessness Quiz – continued

When the teacher is picking on me in class:

a) I try discussing the issue with the teacher, and if that doesn't work, I seek other assistance
b) I try different strategies to change the situation
c) I stop doing my work
d) I seek revenge.

Total your answers

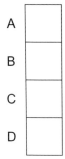

A

B

C

D

Recognising feelings

Recognising the feelings of other people is a social skill that will help you make friends and fit in at school and work, and will help you make decisions about what actions you might take. In fact, having the ability to read emotions is a skill that helps people succeed and enjoy life.

Recognising Feelings

Describe the changes that might occur if a person is:

Angry   Happy   Worried

Facial expression

_____
_____
_____
_____

Body language

_____
_____
_____
_____

Voice

_____
_____
_____
_____

Physical changes

_____
_____
_____
_____

Spoken words

_____
_____
_____
_____

Studying Feelings

What do you think about your feelings? Do you like some feelings, but not others?

Rate these feelings from 1 being 'favourite' to 17 being 'least favourite'.

	happy		sad
	scared		angry
	lonely		loving
	hateful		excited
	helpless		jealous
	calm		bored
	worried		energetic
	belonging		satisfied

Making a plan to master feelings

List the feelings you like most of the time.

_____

_____

List the feelings you often do not like.

_____

_____

Is it a problem if you have feelings you do not like?

_____

_____

Can you make bad feelings go away?

_____

_____

Sometimes you need to have feelings you do not like. They serve an important purpose. Sometimes feelings cause problems. It is a helpful skill to be able to sometimes moderate and even manipulate your feelings. Try to control them, so they do not control you.

For example, being nervous can be a useful feeling. It can act as a warning sign in potentially dangerous situations. It might be telling you to be extra careful.

Being nervous can also be a problem. If you fail to control your nervousness, and you perform below your best, then it is a problem.

Consequently, it is best to accept the feeling of nervousness. Use it to your advantage. If it is causing you problems, try and develop ways of controlling it, so that it does not hinder you from doing your best.

Making decisions about feelings

Which of the feelings expressed in the following situations are helpful, or causing a problem. Is it difficult to know.

Being nervous before a performance.
Being so nervous you perform below your best.
Being nervous when an aggressive person is staring at you.

Being happy when you wake in the morning.
Being happy when you break up with your partner and they cry.

Being sad at a funeral.
Being sad for no particular reason.
Being sad at the ending of a movie.

Being angry with Americans because their leaders declare war.
Being angry with a murderer you have read about in the newspaper.
Being angry with your friend for taking your place on the team.

How can you moderate your feelings?
Do you ever try to influence your feelings?

Controlling your feelings

Think of something that has caused you stress recently.
What did you do?

Answer these questions:
>What was the problem?
>What did you do about it?
>What if the same thing happened to your best friend?
>What advice would you give them?

Recognising thoughts

Sometimes when bad things happen you can make them better or worse by the way you choose to think.

For example, you and your friend do a great piece of work and hand it in to your teacher. The teacher gives it back and says you shouldn't have done it together!

How do you feel?

Now take a minute to think about the thoughts that might go through your mind.

What are they?

a) Perhaps I should have listened to the initial instruction better?

If you thought like the person in (a), how would you feel?

Probably still disappointed, but you are already making a plan to do better next time. You are solving the problem. The feeling of disappointment will not hang around and keep you miserable for too long. You are being positive and getting on with life!

b) No matter how hard I try, I can never get it right.

If you thought like the person in (b), how would you feel?

Probably, you would feel disappointed too. But you are blaming yourself. You are giving yourself a great big 'put down'. You are blowing the teacher's response up into a full-blown catastrophe! Responding in this way, does not solve problems. It does not help you to control your disappointment. It makes it into something worse, a feeling of hopelessness.

c) I hate teachers!

If you thought like the person in (c), how would you feel?

Once again, probably disappointed. But you are blaming the teacher, as if it is their fault. Not only are you blaming the teacher who criticised your work, you are blaming all teachers. You are making yourself angry. When you are angry, you are more likely to do silly things, like behave aggressively or be non-co-operative. Next thing, you might find yourself in trouble for a whole lot of other things. Your thoughts have led you down a path to another full-blown catastrophe!

Be your Own Spin Doctor

Spin doctors make a living putting a positive interpretation on events. They are publicists who often work for famous people. When something happens, they think about the general impression they want to give. In other words, they ask the question, 'What sort of spin do we want to put on this event?'

Whether you are positive or negative, optimistic or pessimistic, often depends on the spin you put on yourself. Choose the spin you would be most likely to put on each of the following events.

If you took your friend's bike without asking and crumpled the front wheel going over a jump, would you think of it as:

a)   a terrible crime where you are exposed as a fraud and a thief
b)   a mistake for which you could be accused of committing a crime
c)   an experiment in poor behaviour that went wrong
d)   an accident that was very unfortunate but nobody's fault.

If you got a low mark in a Maths test, would you put it down as:

a)   evidence that you should give up maths since you are so stupid
b)   a disappointment, since you would have liked to pass but you weren't smart enough
c)   a warning that you need to concentrate harder when the teacher is explaining how to do maths
d)   a motivation to do more homework and show how smart you can actually be.

If you had a crush on someone who already had a partner, would you consider it:

a)   another disaster in a love life strewn with disasters
b)   a stroke of cruel luck that condemns you to a sad and lonely life
c)   a challenge to control your disappointment and move on
d)   an opportunity to lure your crush away from her present partner.

Be Your Own Spin Doctor

If you volunteered to take the final shot in a shoot-out, and missed, would you consider yourself:

- a) so humiliated you could hardly look your team mates in the face
- b) so unskilled you would never take another shot again
- c) unlucky because you knew you were good enough to make the shot
- d) courageous enough to have taken responsibility when it counted.

If your parent was late and missed your part in the school performance, would you believe their behaviour to be:

- a) typically selfish since they are always late
- b) completely thoughtless in failing to realise how disappointed you would be
- c) confusing and inexplicable since they would have been very keen to witness your moment of greatness
- d) obviously caused by misfortune like a serious illness in the family or a flat tyre.

If your friend made a wise-crack when the head teacher was giving your class a serious lecture, would you think they were:

- a) an insolent person who should learn their place
- b) a total lunatic who is destined for serious hardship
- c) a risk-taker who would do well to learn a bit about timing
- d) a very funny person who manages to turn the most painful experiences into something enjoyable.

Count up your answers

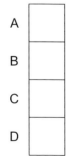

A

B

C

D

Just to complicate matters – the thoughtful optimist

Being positive or optimistic sometimes requires you to 'gild the lily' a little. In other words, to interpret yourself and others in the best possible way.

This does not mean being dishonest. Using the first example where you crash your friend's bike, optimistic thinking should not hinder you from realising your mistake. The thoughtful optimist might forgive themselves, offer to fix the bike and decide never to borrow things without asking. But they would learn. Otherwise their optimism might turn into thoughtlessness or selfishness. They would become an optimist with no friends and no heart.

Spin doctoring stress

Imagine you are at a party. The answer to your dreams is staring at you. When you made it obvious you have noticed, you receive a long and seductive smile in return. You are a bit shaky, you have sweaty palms and your breathing is faster than usual.

Are you nervous and worried? (Negative spin.)

Or are you hopeful and excited? (Positive spin.)

Remember that stress can arise from good events as well as bad ones. Your body's response to a situation may be similar whether you are excited, nervous or angry. The way you an interpret an event may determine whether your stress motivates or cripples you, whether it causes happiness or pain, whether it makes you feel tried or inspired, whether it is good or bad.

Giving compliments

A good start is giving compliments. Begin by noticing things other people do, and saying 'Thank you', 'That was generous', 'You're looking good', 'Hey, I like your smile.'

Try humour

Having a laugh is a great tonic. If someone is laughing, laugh along. Find things that make you giggle like funny movies, cartoons, friends or pets. Remember, feelings are gullible. They believe what you feed them.

Be positive

Some people think people should be realistic, rather than positive. Shouldn't you be honest with yourself? Being realistic is okay. But it is also a little mundane. It doesn't really inspire people or encourage them. Being positive is better. Positive has a secret and magic ingredient that makes life better.

Being positive is laced with hope.

Discover what you like doing

Keep searching for healthy new experiences and challenges that you enjoy and make you feel better. And treasure those things that you already enjoy. Do not forget them. They are too hard to find in the first place.

Participate in rituals

So you are tired of going with your family to Aunt Ettie's for Christmas. Well, complain all you like, but do not stop going. While Aunt Ettie's may not offer much in the way of 'sex, drugs and techno music', the ritual offers plenty of belonging and security.

Block put-downs

Stop yourself from putting yourself down. And do not believe the put-downs from others. When they occur, do not let them pass unchallenged. Explore other ways of thinking. Try and develop the habit of having a positive and optimistic view of yourself and other people.

Make up a mantra for yourself

Just like Nike have a slogan, 'Just do it!' and Toyota have a slogan, 'Oh what a feeling!' Create your own personal reassurance or sales pitch like, 'I'm smart, don't start', 'I can recite prose through my nose', 'Sit tight, I'm alight', 'Don't alarm, it's my charm', 'Get real banana peel', 'Huffy 'n' puffy, I'm like Buffy', 'Lookin' good, Robin Hood', 'Don't weep, breath deep' and so on. While your mantra might help to motivate you, saying it repeatedly may be soothing, and will help you to block the negative thoughts in your head.

Warning signs

When you are being critical of anything and everything, it is time to stop. Turn your thinking around. Stop the criticism. Look for positives. Force out nice comments, even about those who irritate you.

Avoid unrealistic expectations

Try not to put the bar so high that you cannot reach it. Make your goals achievable. Try and do things one step at a time. Remember, if you are not the best, you are with the overwhelming majority.

Build in a circuit breaker

If you are in a rut, do something different. Take on a challenge. Be nice to your pet. Give your mother a compliment. Suggest visiting Great Auntie Ettie.

Well perhaps not Auntie Ettie, but you probably get the idea anyway. Just like for spontaneous eruptions and tooth rattlers, doing something pleasant and engaging will help to give you a break from unpleasant feelings and negative thoughts.

Talk to someone

Talk is a great healer.

Mysteries

One of the great mysteries is that a feeling comes and goes for no particular reason. First thing to remember is that it does go. The quicker the better. You can help it along its way.

A common time people get feelings for no particular reason is when they wake in the morning. For instance, you wake up and you feel miserable. Does it ever happen to you?

Just like the suggestions for how to deal with feelings that are related to thoughts, feelings that come from nowhere can be controlled or moderated by using many of the same techniques as already explained.

And remember, while rotten feelings may seem to come from nowhere, they are just as likely to suddenly disappear to nowhere. One morning you wake up and they are gone.

Grief

What is it?

Grief is your response to a feeling of loss.

Loss can occur in many ways.

Death; the divorce of parents; a betrayal by friends; a separation from friends; a relationship break-up; a disfigurement; loss of pride; loss of status; moving house; starting at a new school; losing your money; losing your pet; or losing a source of enjoyment are some of the things that may cause feelings of loss.

How does it feel?

Everybody experiences grief differently.

You may experience a feeling for a short period of time, every now and again, or every day. Sometimes the period that grief lasts depends on how important the loss. For instance, the loss of a sporting match may not cause as much grief as the loss of a pet.

When you are experiencing grief, you may have many different feelings, sometimes more than one might occur at the same time. You might feel sadness and anger for a time, and then have a moment of joy and hope, only too soon after feel confused and frustrated. Other times you may have to endure the same feeling for a long period of time.

Some nights you may not be able to sleep, and the next night you might sleep like a log. One time you want to talk, and another you want to be withdrawn. One moment you might be restless, another crying and another laughing.

At times you may wish to remain still while experiencing physical discomfort that is caused by stress, and at other times you may want to be doing a physical activity like riding a skateboard or practising ballet.

Do not be frightened. These are all normal reactions.

Grief is a process all people must go through before rediscovering hope and the way ahead.

What can you do about it?

When you suffer loss, grief is a necessary process that you experience. Some people will attempt to avoid it. Do not put your grief on hold for too long. You might find it re-emerges at a time when you are least prepared.

Asking questions and getting information

Wanting answers about a loss is natural and helps us to cope. Some people will want to know immediately, while others may prefer to wait. Do not be afraid to ask questions. Knowing why, what, how and when will help you to understand and begin the process of accepting your loss.

Showing your feelings

Feelings serve a purpose. They help you to recover from loss. You might want to talk to someone. Or you might prefer to do nothing. You might behave unusually. You might play sport, or ride your skateboard, or ballet dance, or sing, or pray, or doing something else that suits you. All of these feelings and reactions are normal. They help you to accept your loss.

Having a daily routine

Building in little anchors to your day like taking the dog for a walk, tidying your room, walking to school with a friend, doing some exercise or another physical activity will help provide a sense of safety and security.

Making sense of your loss and seeking help

A time will come when you consider how your loss has affected your view of life. You will do this partly by reflecting alone, and partly by talking to people you love and trust. Sometimes you need to recognise those who care about you, ask for their help and accept their kindness.

Acknowledgement to Kaye Dennis for content and advice for this section on grief.

Recreational Drugs: Alcohol and Tobacco

Recreational drugs provide people with gratification in exchange for very little effort. This is why they are so enticing. You can use them and soon feel their pleasant effects.

Unpleasant effects

Unfortunately, recreational drugs also have unpleasant effects. If their use gets out of control, they can have adverse consequences. In some cases, they can ruin lives.

Controlling use

Most people limit their use of recreational drugs so that they do not cause problems. They manage to do this because they have developed the skills of impulse control. Rather than using recreational drugs each time the impulse tickles their fancy, they plan how and when they will use drugs.

They also demonstrate the skill of delayed gratification by planning the role they want drugs to have in their life, by making a plan and sticking to it.

Sometimes this might be an informal plan. For instance, some people limit their drinking to one or two glasses of wine with the evening meal. Others might only drink alcohol on special social occasions. Many students make a rule that they will only use alcohol if they are not going to school or studying the next day.

Recreational drugs are seductive

Being aware of their powers of seduction will help you to control them before they begin causing problems.

Two common recreational drugs are alcohol and tobacco. Some information is included to help you consider what role you want them to play in your life: one of pleasure, or ultimately one of regret.

Describe an incident made worse or caused by alcohol. It can be true or make believe.

Describe what you or others might have done to prevent the incident.

Make a list of ideas for reducing risks of alcohol problems in the future.

List the ideas from easiest to hardest for you to begin doing.

Alcohol Quiz

Choose the answer that best represents what you think.

Do you normally use alcohol:
- a) never?
- b) to have fun?
- c) to gain confidence?
- d) to forget?

Do you normally:
- a) abstain while others are drinking?
- b) stop after a few drinks?
- c) drink more than you planned?
- d) drink more than everybody else?

Do you have arguments when using alcohol:
- a) never?
- b) sometimes?
- c) more than other times?
- d) frequently?

Have you had a physical fight when using alcohol:
- a) never?
- b) once?
- c) sometimes?
- d) frequently?

Do you get hangovers:
- a) never?
- b) only rarely?
- c) sometimes?
- d) often?

Count your responses

A ☐   B ☐   C ☐   D ☐

Alcohol Quiz Answers

a)   answers indicate you avoid alcohol.
b)   answers indicate you sometimes have increased risks when using alcohol. Complete the following exercise to plan for minimising harms.
c/d) Answers indicate you are at risk of harm from using alcohol. Complete the exercise on the following page and consider talking to someone you trust about your alcohol use.

Alcohol Damage Quiz

The more ticked boxes, the more difficulties alcohol is possibly causing in your life. If you have a lot of ticked boxes, you might consider discussing your answers with someone you trust.

Alcohol Damage

Tick the word in the left hand column to complete the sentence in the middle and right columns, if it is applicable to your experience with alcohol.

Factor	Alcohol has been a factor when I have had a problem with…	Alcohol has been a factor when one of my friends/ parents has had a problem with…
Violence		
Conflict		
Hangovers		
Committing crime		
Family		
Relationships		
School work		
Employment		
Driving		
Physical injury		
Feeling confused		
Mixing drugs		
Accidents		
Depression		
Worrying		
Anger		
Sleeplessness		
Embarrassment		
Memory		
My reputation		

Tobacco Nicotine Dependence Quiz

Do you think smoking is?
- a) a dangerous habit
- b) something you might try out of curiosity
- c) something that seems enjoyable
- d) something that you are likely to do.

How many cigarettes have you smoked in your lifetime?
- a) None
- b) 1 – 10
- c) 11 – 99
- d) 100+

Do you smoke alone?
- a) never
- b) once or twice
- c) sometimes
- d) often.

When you think of a cigarette do you?
- a) think 'yuk'
- b) quickly forget about it
- c) plan to have one
- d) light up as soon as possible.

If you are at a party, do you?
- a) never smoke
- b) smoke to be sociable
- c) always take cigarettes
- d) smoke more than usual.

Count your responses:

A [ ]   B [ ]   C [ ]   D [ ]

Nicotine Dependence Quiz Answers

a) answers indicate you have avoided smoking. Well done. It is a habit that most people develop against their intentions. Nicotine is a highly addictive ingredient.

b) answers indicate that you have experimented with tobacco, perhaps to be sociable. You are like most people. Be careful, most people become smokers against their intentions. As soon as you begin smoking, you become increasingly sensitive to nicotine. The more you experiment, the more you will have the desire to smoke.

c/d) answers indicate that you are dependent on cigarettes. Nicotine dependence is a difficult habit to break. If you want to learn more about stopping, look at www.givingupsmoking.co.uk

Quitting – anything is possible!

Be aware that…
>   Most people have to try quitting more than once.
>   If you slip, do not lose hope.
>   Keep trying.
>   You will succeed!

Motivate yourself - start thinking of the damage tobacco is doing.

Be positive…
>   Think about being smoke-free.
>   Think about feeling healthy.
>   Think about not having to go outside all the time.
>   Think about controlling your own movements, rather than planning to satisfy a dependence.
>   Think about being free.

Be honest…
>   Think of the gunk in your lungs.
>   Think of a gross tobacco cough.
>   Think of stained teeth.
>   Think of the inconvenience smoking causes you.
>   Think of how you are being controlled by a drug.
>   Think – I am going to succeed with quitting!

Quitting is hard. Quitting needs a plan.

Quitting ideas…

What might be good strategies to give up smoking?

- Get rid of all cigarettes.
- Change your routine. Avoid those things you associate with smoking.
- Drink loads of water and eat plenty of healthy food.
- Do things to take your mind off smoking.
- Do plenty of exercise.
- Avoid smoking situations.
- Avoid triggers; some common ones are: alcohol; stress; tiredness; hunger; caffeine.
- Take one day at a time.
- Don't look for excuses.
- Be positive.
- Ask your friends for their support.
- Have someone to talk to.
- Don't give up, giving up. Quitting often takes many attempts.

Remember, each time you want a cigarette, the urge will last for about five minutes. For the first two+ minutes, the urge will become greater, and then it will begin to ease. How often these urges occur, will depend on how much you smoked and when you stopped. The more you smoked, the more common the urges.

The longer you resist smoking, the further apart the urges will become. They will quickly reduce to a few times a day. Eventually you will hardly ever (if at all) get the urge to smoke. Then you will be free of your dependence.

And you will have proved you can do just about anything!

Appendix

We have provided examples of front covers that could be provided for young people to complete. This age group might prefer to design their own front cover. There is also an open-ended evaluation form that can be used at any stage of the programme.

Managing the
Difficult Emotions

Name _____

Managing the Difficult Emotions

Name _____

Evaluation Form

Date _____

Title of section _____

What was the best part of the session?

_____
_____
_____
_____

What was the worst part of the session?

_____
_____
_____
_____

Today I learned

_____
_____
_____
_____

I'm going to think about

_____
_____
_____
_____

I'll consider changing this part of me

_____
_____
_____
_____

Bibliography

Adler, A. (1943) *Understanding Human Nature*, London, Allen and Unwin.

Armstrong, T. (1999) *Seven Kinds of Smart: Identifying and Developing Your Intelligences*, Plume, USA.

Benard, B. (1991) in *Growing Up In Australia: The Role of Parents in Promoting Positive Adolescent Development* (1999), Commonwealth Department of Family and Community Services, Australia.

Butler, K. (1997) The anatomy of resilience, *Family Therapy Networker*, March/April, 22-31.

Catalano, R. (1997) *Promoting the potential of young people: Communities that Care*, Paper presented in Melbourne, May.

Csikszentmihalyi, M. (1990) *Flow: The Psychology of Optimal Experience*, New York: Harper Collins.

Compas, B., Hinden, B.R. & Gerhardt, C.A. (1995) Adolescent Development: Pathways of risk and resilience, *Annual Review of Psychology*, 46, 265-93.

Covey, S. (1998) *The 7 Habits of Highly Effective Teens,* Simon and Schuster, New York.

Covey, S.R. (1990) *The 7 Habits of Highly Effective People: Powerful Lessons in Personal Change*, Simon and Schuster, New York.

Frydenberg, E. (1997) *Adolescent Coping Theoretical and Research Perspectives*, Routledge, New York.

Frydenberg, E. (editor) *Learning to Cope; Developing as a Person in Complex Societies*, (1999) Oxford university Press, UK

Fuller, A. (1998) *From Surviving to Thriving: Promoting Mental Health in Young People*, Australian Council for Educational Research, Melbourne.

Fuller, A. (2002) *Raising Real People – Creating a Resilient Family*, Melbourne - Australian Council for Educational Research Press.

Fuller, A. (2001) Creating Resilient Learners, *Learning Matters*, 6,3,22- 25.

Gibson-Cline, J.; *Adolescence from Crisis to Coping: A Thirteen Nation Study*, Butterworth-Heineman Ltd, 1996

Goleman, D, (1996) *Emotional Intelligence*, Bloomsbury, London.

Goleman, D, (1998) *Working with Emotional Intelligence*, Bloomsbury, London.

Johnson, R.A. (1989) *Ecstacy*, San Francisco, Harper.

Johnson, R.A. (1993) *Owning Your Own Shadow,* San Francisco, Harper.

Lang, J. (2002) *Re: Life*, Prentice Hall, Australia.

Rayner, M. & Montague, M. (1999) *Resilient Children and Young People*, Deakin Human Services, Australia, Deakin University.

Resnick, M.D., Harris, L.J., & Blum, R.W.(1993) The impact of caring and connectedness on adolescent health and well-being, *Journal of Paediatrics and Child Health*, 29 (Suppl. 1), S3-S9.

Seligman, M. (1993) *What You Can Change and What You Can't: Learning to Accept Who You Are*, Random House, USA.

Seligman, M., Reivich, K., Jaycox, L. & Gillham, J. (1995) *The Optimistic Child*, Random House, Australia.

Shaw, P. (2002) Challenges and Complexities in School Leadership: Finding the Courage to Lead, *Australian Conference on School Leadership*, University of Wollongong, NSW, Australia, March, 2002.

Sternberg, R.J. (2001) Why schools should teach for wisdom: the balance theory of wisdom in educational settings? *Educational Psychologist*, 36, 4, 227-245.

Taylor, S., Pham, L., Rivkin, I. & Armor, D. (1998) Harnessing the imagination: mental stimulation, self-regulation and coping, *American Psychologist*, 53, 429-439.

Young-Eisendrath, P. (1996) *The Resilient Spirit*, Allen and Unwin, Australia.

Van Slyck, M., Stern, M. & Zak-Place, J. (1996) Promoting optimal adolescent development through conflict resolution education, training and practice, *The Counselling Psychologist*, 24 (3), 433-461.

Managing the Difficult Emotions